THE BASICS OF

WINNING HOLD'EM POKER

Avery Cardoza

Cardoza Publishing

Cardoza Publishing is the foremost gaming publisher in the world with a library of more than 175 up-to-date and easy-to-read books and strategies. These authoritative works are written by the top experts in their fields and with more than 8,500,000 books in print, these books represent the best-selling and most popular gaming books anywhere.

FIRST EDITION

Copyright © 2006 by Avery Cardoza
-All Rights Reserved-

Library of Congress Catalog Card Number: 2005920553
ISBN: 1-58042-164-4

Visit our website—www.cardozapub.com—or write for a full list of Cardoza books and advanced strategies.

CARDOZA PUBLISHING
P.O. Box 1500, Cooper Station, New York, NY 10276
Phone (800)577-WINS
email: cardozapub@aol.com
www.cardozapub.com

Table of Contents

ABOUT THE AUTHOR

Avery Cardoza is the world's foremost authority on gambling, a multimillion-selling author of 21 books, and the publisher of the acclaimed national gambling lifestyle magazine, *Avery Cardoza's Player*. His books include *Poker Talk*, *The Basics of Winning Poker*, *How to Play Winning Poker* and *Crash Course in Beating Texas Hold'em Poker*.

He is a frequent money-winner and regular player in the high stakes poker tournaments seen on television. Cardoza has crippled the stacks of, or eliminated, more than a dozen world champions from major tournament competitions.

I. INTRODUCTION

Texas hold'em, or **hold'em** as the game is more commonly known, is the hot game it seems *everyone* is playing. Fueled by the remarkable success of the World Poker Tour, the highly publicized run of an unknown player to a World Championship title, and the explosion of online poker, the game has become enormously popular.

In this book, we'll cover two forms of hold'em: limit hold'em, which is the predominate form of hold'em played for cash in cardrooms and casinos, and no-limit hold'em, played in both cash games and in the very popular tournaments—and not just the local ones you can play for thousands and tens of thousands in prize money, but the big events with millions of dollars at stake!

This book will get you started in this very exciting game. We'll go over all the basics of play so you can step right in and join the very exciting world of poker. You'll also learn the winning strategies for limit, no-limit, and tournament hold'em and then how to put all the pieces together and walk away with money in your pocket.

With a little luck and some skill, you can be on your way to fame and fortune.

Let's get started!

II. OVERVIEW

Your final five-card hand in hold'em will be made up of the best five-card combination of the seven total cards available to you. These include the **board**, five cards dealt face-up in the middle of the table, cards which are shared by all players, and your **pocket cards** or **hole cards**, two cards dealt face-down that can be used by you alone. For example, your final hand could be composed of your two pocket cards and three cards from the board, one pocket card and four from the board, or simply all five board cards.

At the beginning of a hand, each player is dealt two face-down cards. Then each player gets a chance to exercise his betting options. Next, three cards are dealt simultaneously on the table for all players to share. This is called the **flop**, and it is followed by another round of betting. A fourth board card, called the **turn**, is then dealt, and it too is followed by a round of betting. One final community card is dealt in the center of the table, making five total. This is the **river**. If two or more players remain in the hand, it is followed by the fourth and final betting round.

When all bets have concluded, there is the **showdown**, where the highest ranking hand in play wins the **pot**—the accumulation of bets that are kept in the center of the table. The pot can also be won by a player when all of his opponents fold their hands at any point before the showdown, leaving one player alone to claim the pot—even though he may not actually have held the best hand!

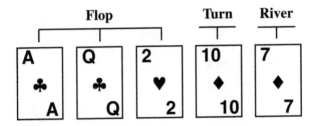

III. TYPES OF HOLD'EM GAMES

Hold'em can be played in two basic ways—as a cash game or in a tournament format.

CASH GAMES

In a **cash game**, the chips you play with represent real money. If you go broke, you can always dig in to your pocket for more money. If you give the poker room $200 in cash, you get $200 worth of chips in return. If you build it up to $375, you can quit and convert your chips to cash anytime you want.

Your goal in a cash game is to win as much money as you can, or if things are going poorly, at least to lose as little as possible.

TOURNAMENT HOLD'EM

In a **tournament**, every player starts with an equal number of chips and plays until one player holds them all. Your goal in a tournament is to survive as long as you can. At the very least, you want to survive long enough to earn prizes, usually money, and in the best case scenario, to win it all, become the champion, and win the biggest prize.

As players lose their chips, they are eliminated from the tournament. Unlike a cash game, where the chips are the equivalent of cash money, **tournament**

chips are only valuable in the tournament itself and have no cash value.

LIMIT, NO-LIMIT, AND POT-LIMIT

Hold'em, or any form of poker for that matter, has three different types of betting structures: limit, pot-limit, and no-limit. These structures don't change the basic way the games are played, only the amount of money that can be bet.

The big difference between the three structures is the strategy. The amount you can bet changes the hands that you should play, when you should play them, and how much you should risk in any given situation.

Let's take a look at each betting structure.

Limit Poker

In **limit poker**, the most common game played in cardrooms and casinos for cash, all bets are divided into a two-tier structure, such as $3/$6, $4/$8, $5/$10, and $15/$30, with the larger limit bets being exactly double the lower limit. On the preflop and flop, all bets and raises must be at the lower limit, and on the turn and river, all bets double and are made at the higher limit. Unless a player is short-stacked and cannot meet the required amount, all bets must be at the preestablished limits of the game.

One form of limit poker, called **spread-limit**, allows you to bet any amount between the minimum and maximum amounts specified for the game. Spread limit is typically played in very low stakes games. For example, in a $1-$5 game, you may bet or raise $1, $2, $3, $4, or $5 before the flop, or on the flop, turn or river. There is also a $1-$4-$8 spread-limit format where all bets on the preflop and flop can be anywhere from $1 to $4, and on the turn, and river, from $1 to $8.

No-Limit Poker

No-limit hold'em is the exciting no-holds barred style of poker played in the World Series of Poker main event and seen on television by millions weekly on the World Poker Tour and stations such as The Travel Channel and ESPN. The prevailing feature of no-limit hold'em is that you can bet any amount up to what you have in front of you on the table *anytime* it is your turn. That exciting all-in call signals a player's intention to put all his chips on the line.

Pot-Limit Poker

Pot-limit, the least popular of the three structures, is a blend between limit and no-limit. The minimum bet allowed in pot-limit is that of the big blind bet (which helps determine the size of the game), while the maximum bet allowed is defined by the size of the *pot*. For example, if $75 is currently in the pot, then $75 is the maximum bet allowed. The pot sizes in pot-limit quickly escalate to large amounts. Like no-limit, this betting structure is not for the timid.

IV. THE POKER SETTING

THE DEALER

In a casino or cardroom, the house will supply a **dealer**. He is not a participant in the betting and play of the game. His role is simply to shuffle the deck, deal the cards, and direct the action so that the game runs smoothly. He will point out whose turn it is to play and pull bets into the pot after each round of cards. And at the showdown, he will declare the winner, push the pot over to the winning player, then reshuffle the cards, and get ready for the next deal.

THE PLAYERS

A typical hold'em game fields between eight and ten players, though as few as two is enough to have a game. More than ten can play, though eleven or more players would be unusual—and crowded.

A cash game with seven or more players is known as a **ring game**. Six players or fewer is considered **short-handed**. And when there are just two players going against one another, it is called a **head-to head** or **heads-up** game.

THE POKER TABLE

In a cardroom, the players and dealer sit around a table built to accommodate the game of poker, and often, specifically hold'em (hold'em tables are larger than seven-card stud tables). The typical hold'em table is oblong and can hold up to ten players seated comfortably. At home, of course, any table can be used.

The dealer sits in the middle of the long side where there is an indentation cut into the table to facilitate access to the players. He will usually have a small rack in front of him where he can keep an extra deck of cards, chips, cash, and a few other items. In a cash game, he may also have a drop box where he will deposit money taken out of the pot as the house commission (see "Rake," next chapter).

CHIPS AND MONEY

Poker is almost always played with **chips**, thin, circular clay or plastic units that are assigned specific values, such as $1, $5, $25, and $100. Poker can also be played for cash, but this is discouraged in cardrooms as it slows down the game. Chips are much more practical to use.

CARDS

Hold'em is played with a standard pack of fifty-two cards consisting of thirteen ranks, ace through king in each of four suits (hearts, clubs, diamonds, spades). The ace is the best and highest card, followed in descending order by the king, queen, jack, 10, 9, 8, 7, 6, 5, 4, 3 and then the 2. When the cards are held together in various combinations, they form hands of different strengths. These are called **hand rankings** or **poker rankings**.

V. POKER FUNDAMENTALS

Hold'em is played as high poker, that is, the player with the highest five-card combination at the showdown will have the winning hand and collect the money in the pot. Of course, if all players but one are out of the pot before the showdown, the remaining player will win regardless of what hand he holds.

OBJECT OF THE GAME

Your goal is to win as many chips as possible. In cash games, this means making as much money as you can, and in a tournament, this means being the last player left after all opponents have been knocked out, making you the biggest prize winner and the champion.

You can win only what your opponents risk, so pots will be of different sizes. They will vary from small ones, in which players have hands they are not willing to commit many chips to, to large ones where two or more players have strong hands they think will win and will push chips at each other in an effort to build the pot or induce opponents to throw away their cards and bow out of the hand.

Do not confuse the goal of winning chips with winning pots. It is not how many pots you win, but how much money. It is better to win one pot with $500 in chips than three pots with $100 each.

In fact, the player who wins the most pots often is a player who ends up a loser! Why? He's playing too many hands, and while he's winning a lot of them, at the same time, he is losing a lot of them.

HAND RANKINGS

The standard poker rankings are used in hold'em. The royal flush is the highest, then the straight flush, four of a kind, full house, flush, straight, three of a kind, two pair, one pair, and then high card. The order in which cards are dealt or how they are displayed is irrelevant to the final value of the hand. For example, 7-7-K-A-5 is equivalent to A-K-7-7-5.

This is how the hands are formed:

High-Card Hands – Hands that have no stronger combinations, such as a pair, two pair or better—simply five odd cards. 3-9-K-7-10, is a "king-high" hand. The highest ranking card in a high card hand, or if tied, the next highest untied card, will beat a lesser high card hand. A-K-J-10-4 beats A-K-J-3-2.

One Pair – Two cards of equal rank. Example: 5-5-8-J-K. If two players are competing with one-pair hands, then the higher ranked of the pairs—aces highest, deuces lowest— wins the pot. And if two players have the same pair, then the highest side card would be used to determine the higher-ranking hand. 5-5-A-7-6 beats 5-5-K-Q-J, since the ace is a higher kicker than the king.

Two Pair – Two pairs and an odd card. Example: 6-6-J-J-2. The highest pair of competing two-pair hands will win, or if the top pair is tied, then the second pair. If both pairs are equivalent, then the fifth card decides the winner. K-K-3-3-6 beats J-J-8-8-Q and K-K-2-2-A, but loses to K-K-3-3-9.

Three of a Kind – Three cards of equal rank and two odd cards. Also called **trips** or a **set**. Example: Q-Q-Q-7-J. If two players hold a set, the higher ranked set will win, and if both players hold an equivalent set, then the highest odd card determines the winner. 7-7-7-4-2 beats 5-5-5-A-K, but loses to 7-7-7-9-5.

Straight – Five cards of mixed suits in sequence, but it may not wrap around the ace. For example, Q-J-10-9-8 of mixed suits is a straight, but Q-K-A-2-3 is not—it's simply an ace-high hand. If two players hold straights, the higher straight card at the top end of the sequence will win. J-10-9-8-7 beats

5-4-3-2-A but would tie another player holding J-10-9-8-7.

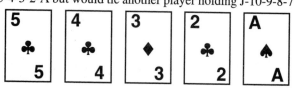

Flush – Five cards of the same suit. Example: K-10-9-5-3, all in diamonds. If two players hold flushes, the player with the highest untied card wins. Suits have no relevance. Thus, Q-J-7-5-4 of diamonds beats Q-J-4-3-2 of spades.

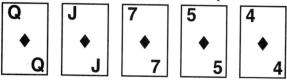

Full House – Three of a kind and a pair. Example: 5-5-5-9-9. If two players hold full houses, the player with the higher three of a kind wins. J-J-J-8-8 beats 7-7-7-A-A.

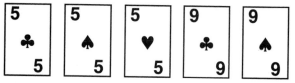

Four of a Kind - Four cards of equal rank and an odd card. Also called **quads.** Example: K-K-K-K-3. If two players hold quads, the higher ranking quad will win the hand. K-K-K-K-3 beats 7-7-7-7-A and K-K-K-K-2.

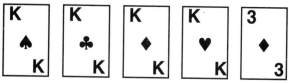

Straight Flush – Five cards in sequence, all in the same suit. Example: 7-6-5-4-3, all in spades. If two straight flushes are competing, the one with the highest card wins.

Royal Flush – The A-K-Q-J-10 of the same suit, the best hand possible. No royal flush is higher than another.

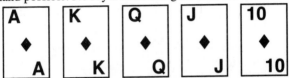

HOW TO READ YOUR HOLD'EM HAND

You have all seven cards available to form your final five-card hand—any combination of your two hole cards and the five cards from the board. You can even use all five board cards. Let's look at an example.

You   **Your Opponent**

The Board

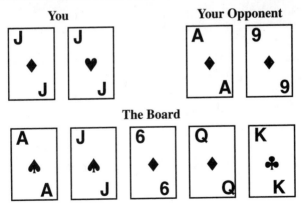

Your best hand, three jacks, is made using your two pocket cards and one jack from the board. This beats your opponent's pair of aces, formed with one card from his hand and one from the board. In both instances, the other cards are not relevant. For example there is no need to say three jacks with an ace and a king versus two aces with a king, queen and jack—simply, three jacks versus two aces.

If the river card, the last card turned up on the board, had been a K♦ instead of a K♣, your opponent would have a diamond flush (formed with his two pocket diamonds and the three diamonds on the board), which would beat your set of jacks.

BETTING OPTIONS

When it is your turn to play, the following options, which apply to all forms of poker, are available to you:

1. Bet: Put chips at risk, that is, wager money, if no player has done so before you.

2. Call: Match a bet if one has been placed before your turn.

3. Raise: Increase the size of a current bet such that opponents, including the original bettor, must put additional money into the pot to stay active in a hand.

4. Fold: Give up your cards and opt out of play if a bet is due and you do not wish to match it. This forfeits your chance of competing for the pot.

5. Check: Stay active in a hand without making a bet and risking chips. This is only possible if no bets have been made.

The first three options—bet, call, and raise—are all a form of putting chips at risk in hopes of winning the pot. Once chips are bet and due, you must match that bet to continue playing for the pot or you must fold. Checking is not an option. If no chips are due, you can stay active in the hand without cost by checking.

When a bet has been made, it no longer belongs to the bettor; it becomes the property of the pot, the communal collection of money that is up for grabs by all active players.

HOW TO BET

A bet is made by either pushing the chips in front of you—an action which speaks for itself—or by verbally calling out the play, and *then* pushing the chips in front of you. Simply announce, "I call," "I bet," "I raise," or whatever clearly indicates your desire, and then push your chips out on the felt. Note that if you announce a bet or a fold, it is binding and you're committed to the action.

Your bet should be placed at least six inches toward the middle, but not so far that your chips mingle with those already in the pot and cannot be distinguished from them. That is, your chips should be far enough away from your own stack and the pot so that they are clearly seen not only as a bet, but as *your* bet.

Do not throw your chips into the actual pot, which is called **splashing the pot**. This protects all players from an opponent intentionally or unintentionally miscalling a bet. Betting properly also allows the amount of the wager to easily be verified while making it clear to all players that a bet or raise has been made.

To check, tap or knock on the table with your fingertips or hand or announce "I check" or "check." To fold, push your cards or toss them *face down* towards the dealer. It is illegal to show your cards to active players who are competing for the pot.

BETTING ETIQUETTE

It is important to wait for your turn to play before announcing or revealing to any opponents what decision you will make. For example, if you know you're going to fold, you shouldn't toss your cards to the dealer before the action comes around to your position. And when you do give up your hand, pass the cards to the dealer face down, so that no other player can view them. If any cards are revealed to any one player, the rules of the game require that all players see them so that everyone is kept on equal footing.

It is improper and illegal to discuss your hand or another player's hand while a game is in progress. It is also very poor form to criticize other players strategy decisions, no matter how poor they appear to be. If you think an opponent plays poorly, then that's good news for you: Go win his chips.

MINIMUM AND MAXIMUM BETS
Limit Poker

The minimum and maximum bets in limit games are strictly regulated according to the preset limits of the game. For example, $3/$6 and $5/$10 are two common limits.

The number of raises allowed in a round are also restricted, usually limited to three or four total according to the house rules for the cardroom. In other words, if there is a three-raise limit and the action goes bet, raise, reraise, and reraise, the raising would be **capped**. No more raises would be allowed for that round.

The exception to this rule comes into play when players are heads-up, in which case, there is no cap to the number of raises that can be made.

No-Limit

In no-limit cash games and tournaments, there is no cap to the number of raises allowed or how high a bet or raise can be. Players may raise to their hearts content or for all their chips.

The minimum bet in no-limit must be at least the size of the big blind. Thus, if the big blind is $5, then the minimum allowed bet is $5. And raises must be at least equal to the size of the previous bet or raise in the round.

For example, a $10 bet can be raised $30 more to make it $40 total. If a succeeding player reraises, he would have to make it at least $30 more—since that is the size of the last raise—for $70 total.

TABLE STAKES, TAPPED OUT PLAYERS, AND SIDE POTS

You may only bet or call bets up to the amount of money you have on the table. This is called **table stakes**. You are not allowed to withdraw money from your wallet, borrow from other players, or receive credit while a hand is in progress. Getting extra cash or chips is permissible only *before* the cards are dealt.

For example, in limit poker, if the bet is $25 and you only have $10, you may only call for $10. The remaining $15 and all future monies bet during this hand—except for bets by opponents to equal the $10—would be separated into a **side pot**. A player who has no more table funds from which to bet is **tapped-out**.

A tapped-out player can still receive cards until the showdown and play for the **main pot**, however, he can no longer bet in this hand and has no interest in the side pot. The other active players can continue to bet against each other for the money in the side pot in addition to remaining in competition for the main pot with the tapped-out player.

At the showdown, if the tapped-out player has the best hand, he receives only the money in the main pot. The side pot will be won by the player having the best hand among the remaining players. Should one of the other players hold the overall best hand, that player wins both the original pot and the side pot.

If only one opponent remains when a player taps out, then there is no more betting, and cards are played out until the showdown, where the best hand wins.

THE RAKE

In poker, players compete against one another, not against the house, as in games such as blackjack and craps. Cardrooms act only as a host of poker games and make their money by taking a percentage of each pot, called a **rake**, as their fee for running the game. In low limit games and online, the rake can be anywhere from 5% to 10%, usually with a cap of $3 to $5 per pot. In higher limit games, the house typically charges players by time.

Time collection, where the house charges players by the half-hour or hour, is the preferred method of rakes. Generally speaking, this will come out to a smaller fee than the rakes taken out of the pot. While you generally don't have a choice given that you'll be playing where you'll be playing, you should be aware of the size rake that a cardroom collects, as it greatly impacts your profit potential. The rake, in a sense, serves as a tax. Obviously, the lower the rake, the better it is for your bottom line.

In tournaments, the house rake is collected up-front. For example, a tournament with a $500 entry fee may add $40 to the $500 so your real cost might be $540. The $500 goes into the prize pool for the players, while the $40 goes to the dealers as a tip and the house for its fee.

VI. THE PLAY OF THE GAME

All play and strategy in hold'em depends upon the position of the **button**, which is a small disk, typically plastic and labeled "Dealer." The player who has the button in front of him, who is also known as the button, will have the advantage of acting last in every round of betting except for the preflop round. After each hand is completed, the disk rotates clockwise to the next player.

The player immediately to the left of the button is called the **small blind** and the one to his left is called the **big blind**. These two players are required to post bets, called **blinds**, before the cards are dealt.

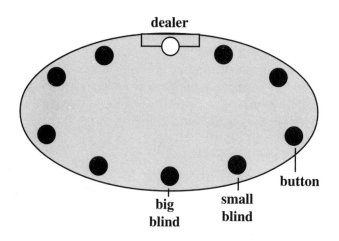

The big blind is typically the same size as the lower bet in a limit structure, so if you're in a $3/$6 game, the big blind would be $3 and in a $5/$10 game, it would be $5. The small blind will either be half the big blind in games where the big blind evenly divides to a whole dollar, or two-thirds of the big blind when it doesn't. For example, the small blind might be $10 in a $15/$30 game and $2 in a $3/$6 game.

In no-limit cash games, the amount of the blinds are preset and remain constant throughout the game. Typical blinds for cash games might be $2/$5, $3/$5 or $5/$10 for the small blind and big blind respectively. Bigger blinds mean more action and larger games.

In tournaments, however, the blinds steadily increase as the event progresses, forcing players to play boldly to keep up with the greater costs of the blinds.

ANTES

Antes are mandatory bets that every player must make before the cards are dealt and are in addition to the blinds. They are only required in tournaments after some rounds have been played (see Tournament Poker chapter). There are no antes in cash hold'em games.

ORDER OF BETTING

Play always proceeds clockwise around the table. On the preflop, the first betting round, the first player to the left of the big blind goes first. He can call the big blind to stay in competition for the pot, raise, or fold. Every player following him has the same choices: call, raise, or fold. The last player to act on the preflop is the big blind. If no raises have preceded his turn, the big blind can either end the betting in the round by calling, or he can put in a raise. However, if there are any raises in the round, the big blind and other remaining players must call or raise these bets to stay active, or they must fold.

On the other betting rounds—the flop, turn and river—the first active player to the button's left will go first and the player on the button will go last. If the button has folded, the player sitting closest to his right will act last. When all bets and raises have been met on the flop and turn, or if all players check, then the next card will be dealt. On the river, after all betting action is completed, players will reveal their cards to see who has the best hand.

Betting in a round stops when the last bet or raise has been called and no bets or raises are due any player. Players cannot raise their own bets or raises.

At any time before the showdown, if all opponents fold, then the last active player wins the pot.

SAMPLE GAME

Let's follow the action in a sample $3/$6 limit game with nine players so that you can see how hold'em is played.

In limit poker, the betting structure has two levels, the lower levels being the amount you must bet or raise on the preflop and flop ($3 in a $3/$6 game), and the higher levels being the amount you must bet or raise on the turn and river ($6 in a $3/$6 game).

A no-limit game would proceed *exactly* like the sample limit hold'em game shown below—the same order of play and the same options are available to the players. The only difference is that there is no cap to the amount that can be bet. Players can bet or raise any amount greater than the minimum allowed, up to all their chips, when it is their turn.

The Deal

Before the cards are dealt, the small blind and the big blind must post their bets. Once that occurs, the dealer will distribute cards one at a time, beginning with the small blind, who is the player sitting to the immediate left of the button, and proceeding clockwise until all players have received two face down cards.

The Preflop

The player to the big blind's left acts first. He has the option of calling the $3 big blind bet, raising it $3 more, or folding. Checking is not an option on the preflop as there is already a bet on the table—the $3 big blind bet.

Let's say this player folds. The next player is faced with the same decisions: call, raise, or fold. He calls for $3. Since this is a $3/$6 game, all bets and raises in this round *must* be in $3 increments. The next three players fold. The following player raises $3, making it

$6 total—the $3 call plus the $3 raise.

It is the button's turn, the player sitting in the dealer position. He thinks about his cards and calls the $6. Now it is up to the small blind. The small blind has already put in $2 so he must put in $4 more to play. If there had been no raise, it would cost him just $1 more to meet the $3 big blind bet and stay active.

The small blind folds and the big blind considers reraising the raiser, but instead just calls the $3 raise. Play now moves back to the original caller. Since he has only put $3 into the pot, he must meet the $3 raise to stay in the hand. He calls and since all bets and raises have been matched, the round is over. We'll see the flop four-handed.

Note that the big blind always has the option to raise on the preflop. The dealer will say "option," on the big blind's turn letting him know he can raise if he wants. If there had been no raises and the big blind calls, the preflop betting is finished for the round. If the big blind raises, then the other active players must meet that raise to stay active.

If all players fold on the preflop, the big blind wins the hand by default.

The Flop

At the conclusion of betting, the dealer pulls the blinds and bets into the pot. He takes the top card off the deck and **burns** it, that is, he removes it from play, and then deals the three card flop face-up in the center of the table.

Bets and raises during this round are still at the $3 level. The first active player to the button's left goes first. Since the small blind has folded, it is the big blind's turn. There are no bets that have to be met—the forced first round blind bet only occurs on the preflop—so the big blind may check or bet. (There is no reason to fold, which would be foolish, as it costs nothing to stay active.)

The big blind checks, the next player checks, the original raiser from the preflop checks, and it is now up to the button. He pushes $3 into the pot forcing the other three players to put up $3 if they want to see another card. The big blind, who checked first in this round, is the next active player. He must call or raise this bet to continue with the hand, or he must fold. He decides to call for $3 and the other two players fold. Since all bets have been called, betting is complete for the round.

We're now heads-up, the big blind versus the button.

The Turn

The dealer burns the top card and then deals a fourth community card face-up on the table. This is known as the **turn** or **fourth street**. Betting moves to the upper limit, so now all bets and raises are in $6 increments. The big blind, being the first active player on the button's left, goes first and checks. The button checks as well. Since all active players checked, the betting round is over.

The River and the Showdown

After the top card is burned, the fifth and final community card is turned over and placed next to the other four cards in the center of the table. Players now have five community cards along with their two pocket cards to form their final five card hand.

At the **river** or **fifth street**, there is one final round of betting. The big blind goes first and leads out with a $6 bet. The button calls, and that concludes the betting since the big blind cannot raise his own bet. We now have the showdown. The big blind turns over K-Q, which combines with a a board of K-Q-10-7-5 for two pair of kings and queens. The button's K-10 also gives him two pair led by kings, but his second pair is tens. The big blind has the superior hand and wins the money in the pot.

Had the button simply folded, the big blind would have won by default, since no other players remained to contest the pot.

On the showdown, the last player to bet or raise (or if there has been no betting in the round, then the first person to the left of the button) has to show his cards first. Losers can simply **muck** their cards, that is, fold them, without showing their cards.

The dealer pushes the chips in the pot over to the winner, collects and shuffles the cards, and prepares to deal a new hand. The button moves clockwise, so the big blind is now the small blind, and the small blind becomes the button.

VII. TOURNAMENT POKER

Tournaments are set up as a process of elimination. As players lose their chips and are eliminated from a tournament, the remaining competitors get consolidated into fewer tables. What might start out as a 200 player event played at twenty ten-handed tables will get reduced to nineteen tables, and then eighteen tables, and so on, as players bust out.

Eventually, the field will get narrowed down to just one table, the **final table**, where the prestige and big money is earned. And that table will play down until just one player is left holding all the chips—the **champion**.

REBUY AND FREEZE-OUT TOURNAMENTS

There are two types of tournaments—freeze-outs and rebuy tournaments. A **freeze-out tournament** is a do or die structure. Once you run out of chips, you are eliminated. Unlike a cash game, you can't go back into your pocket for more chips.

In a **rebuy tournament**, you can purchase additional chips, which is usually allowed only when your chip stack is equal to or less than the original starting amount and only during the first few specified rounds of play. This is called the **rebuy period**. Some tournaments allow limited rebuys, and others allow players to rebuy as often as they go broke, that is, until the rebuy period is over.

At the end of the rebuy period, most tournaments allow you to get an **add-on** as well—a final purchase of a specific amount of additional chips. Usually, only one add-on is permitted per player, though some events allow double add-ons, and rarely, even more.

Once the rebuy period is over, you're playing in pure survival mode. If you lose your chips, you are eliminated and your tournament is over.

COSTS OF ENTERING

Entry fees for tournaments can be anywhere from $10 to $25,000! Tournaments with entry fees under $100 are usually played as rebuy tournaments, while those with buy-ins greater than $1,000 are typically freeze-outs. The bigger money events like the ones you see on television featuring the top pros are almost always freeze-out tournaments.

TOURNAMENT STRUCTURE

Tournaments are divided into **levels** or **rounds**. Each level is marked by an increase in the amount of chips players are forced to commit to the pot before the cards are dealt. The blinds slowly increase, and after a few levels, the antes kick in. Levels may be as short as fifteen or twenty minutes in low buy-in events that are designed to be completed in as little as a few hours, or as long as ninety minutes to two hours for major events that are structured to last up to a week.

Typically, every ninety minutes or two hours in a tournament, you will be given a ten or fifteen minute break.

TOURNAMENT CHIPS

Unlike a cash game, where chips are the exact equivalent of money, tournament chips have no cash value. They may just as well be Monopoly money, because no one is going to give you anything for them outside the tournament. Thus, if you have accumulated $150,000 in tournament chips and try to cash them out, all you'll get from the casino is an incredulous look and an explanation that all you have are tournament chips.

TOURNAMENT PRIZE POOL

Most tournaments are set up so that approximately 10%-15% of all players (and sometimes as high as 20%) will win cash prizes. The number of paid places, those who finish **in the money**, is decided in advance by the organizers.

The greater the number of players, the bigger the prize pool. When the events are large, such as the $10,000 buy-in events, the prize pool often gets into the millions.

VIII. SEVEN KEY STRATEGIC CONCEPTS

The following key concepts apply to all forms of hold'em.

1. RESPECT POSITION
In hold'em, where you sit relative to the button is called **position**. In a nine-handed game, the first three spots to the left of the button are known as **early position**, the next three, **middle position**, and the last three, **late position**. In a ten-handed game, early position is the four spots to the left of the button.

The later the position, the bigger the advantage, because you get to see what your opponents do before deciding whether to commit any chips to the pot. The earlier the position, the more vulnerable your hand is to being raised and thus the more powerful your hand must be for you to enter the pot.

In late position, you have more options and leverage so you can play more hands. If the early betting action is aggressive, you can fold marginal hands without cost. And if the betting action is weak, you can be more aggressive with marginal hands and see the flop with better position.

2. PLAY GOOD STARTING CARDS

You must start out with good cards to give yourself the best chance to win. And while this seems obvious, you'd be surprised at the number of players who ignore this basic strategic concept and take loss after loss by chasing inferior and losing hands. If you play too many hands in poker, you'll soon find yourself without chips. Enter the pot with good starting cards in the right position and you give yourself good chances to finish with winners.

3. PLAY OPPONENTS

By watching how an opponent plays, you get all sorts of information on how to take advantage of his tendencies. For example, when a player infrequently enters a pot, he's **tight**, and you can often force him out of hands even when he may have better cards than you. You'll give him credit for big hands when he's in a pot, and get out of his way unless you have a big hand yourself.

On the other hand, an opponent who plays a lot of hands is **loose**, and you can figure him for weaker cards on average. You also need to adjust for **aggressive** players, who often raise when they get involved in a pot and **passive** players, opponents you can play against with less fear of getting raised.

4. BE THE AGGRESSOR

Hold'em is a game where aggression brings the best returns. It's almost always better to raise than to call. Raising immediately puts pressure on opponents who will often fold right there, unwilling to commit chips to their marginal hands. Or they will see the flop but will be ready to drop out against further bets if it doesn't connect strongly enough with their cards—which happens most of the time.

5. WIN CHIPS, NOT POTS

You want to win chips and to do so, you need to win pots, particularly big ones if you can. So keep this in mind: It is not the quantity of pots you win, but the quality of them that matters.

6. FOLD LOSING HANDS

Part of winning is minimizing losses when you have the second best hand. This means not chasing pots when you are a big underdog to win, especially longshot draws against heavy betting. You can't win them all. Save your chips for better opportunities. Cutting losses on hands you lose adds to overall profits.

7. PATIENCE

Hold'em is a game of patience. You will often go long stretches between good hands. Winning players exercise patience and wait for situations where they can win chips. Your good hands will come, and if you haven't blown yourself out trying to force plays, you'll be able to take advantage of them and win some nice pots for yourself.

IX. LIMIT HOLD'EM STRATEGY

In limit hold'em, where all betting is in a two-tier structure, such as $3/$6 or $5/$10, the three main factors to consider when deciding how to play a hand are the strength of your starting cards, where you are sitting relative to the button, and the action that precedes your play. There are other considerations that enter into the mix, such as the cost of entering the pot and the aggressiveness or tightness of the table, but you should always consider these three fundamental factors first.

STARTING CARDS

The biggest mistake novices and habitually losing players make in hold'em is playing too many hands. Each call costs at least one bet. They compound this mistake when they catch a piece of the flop—but not enough of it—leading to more inadvisable bets and raises when they are holding a losing hand, thus making the situation even more costly. These lost chips add up quickly and set the stage for losing sessions.

So the foundation of playing winning hold'em is starting with solid cards, that is, playing the right cards in the right positions.

We'll divide the starting hands into four different categories: Premium, Playable, Marginal, and Junk.

PREMIUM STARTING HANDS

A-A K-K A-K Q-Q J-J

Limit hold'em is a game of big cards. Aces, kings, queens, jacks, and A-K are the best starting hands. They are strong enough to raise from any position at the table and should be played aggressively. You hope to accomplish two things with the raise. First, you want to get more money into the pot on a hand in which you're probably leading, and second, you want to protect that hand by narrowing the field of opponents.

The greater the number of players who stay in the pot, the greater the chances that a weaker hand will draw out and beat your premium hand.

If a player raises ahead of you or reraises behind you, reraise with aces and kings, and just call with the other premium hands and see how the flop goes. Jacks are weaker than the other big pairs because there is about a 50% chance that an overcard, a queen, king, or ace will come on the flop, making your hand vulnerable.

If an overcard flops when you have jacks, queens, or even kings, or you miss entirely with A-K, you have to think about giving up on these hands if an opponent bets into you or check-raises. For example, if the flop is Q-7-6 and you have A-K or J-J, and an opponent leads into you, you're probably donating chips. A better flop would be K-10-3 for A-K or 10-8-2 for J-J.

It's also tough to play high pairs against an ace flop since players will often play starting cards con-

taining an ace. And in low-limit games, you'll get players seeing the flop with all sorts of hands, so if there
are a bunch of players in the pot, you have to be concerned about an ace flopping when you have a big
pocket pair, such as kings. If you have A-K, however,
that flop puts you in a strong position, especially in a
game where opponents like to play ace-anything.

You're also concerned with flops of three con-
necting cards, such as 8-9-10 and three suited cards if
you don't have the ace of the same suit for a powerful
flush draw—four cards of one suit needing one more
card of that suit to complete a flush. These are not good
flops for big pairs or an A-K.

PLAYABLE STARTING HANDS

A-Q   A-J   A-10   K-Q   10-10   9-9   8-8

These starting hands should be folded in early position. They should also be folded in middle or late
position if the pot has been raised from early position,
which suggests strength, unless you think the raiser is
loose and you can see the flop for just that one bet.

If players **limp** into the pot before you—that is, if
they just call the bet—you can limp in as well with the
Playable hands. Sometimes a raise will be good if you
can force out players behind you and isolate the limper.
However, if you're in there against loose players who
are not easily moved off a pot, which will generally be
the case in low limit and internet poker games, you
might consider calling. When you're up against opponents who cannot be chased by raises, you'd prefer to

see the flop for one bet with these hands.

If you enter the pot and it gets raised after you, you have to make a decision. If the raise comes from late position and it's from a loose player, you have more reason to call then to fold. It's just one bet. However, if it's raised twice and costs you two more bets, or it looks like you might be trapped between a bettor and a raiser, get away from these hands while it's still cheap. There is too much strength against you.

What if no one has entered the pot before you? If you're in middle or late position, you should raise coming into the pot and try to limit the field or even better, get the blinds.

MARGINAL STARTING HANDS
7-7   5-5   3-3   6-6   4-4   2-2
K-J   Q-J   K-J   Q-10   K-10   J-10
A-x (ace with any other card)
Suited connectors: 5-6, 6-7, 7-8, 8-9, 9-10

Play marginal hands only if you can get in for one bet—but not at the cost of two bets. This means you'll fold these hands in early and middle position where you are vulnerable to being raised.

In late position, call in an unraised pot, but if the pot has already been raised from early or middle position or you are between a bettor and a raiser, these marginal cards become unprofitable and should be folded.

If there is a raise after you enter the pot, you can

call with these marginal hands—when the cost is only one bet—but fold in the face of a double raise or in situations where yet another raise can follow.

PLAYING LATE POSITION

You can play many more hands from late position. You've had a chance to see the betting before it reaches your position. If the action is heavy, you fold all non-premium hands. If the action is light and the cost is cheap, you can get more creative. And if no one has entered the pot, you should often raise, as there is a good chance no one will call and you'll get the blinds.

If there are only limpers, you add **suited connectors**—hands that are consecutive in rank, such as 5-6 or 8-9, and in the same suit—to your starting hands. Suited connectors are best played in a pot with three or more players. You want multiple opponents in the pot so that you can win a bunch of chips if you hit your hand. If the pot is raised and it would cost you two bets to play, call only if it looks like there will be enough players in to see the flop.

Pairs of twos through sevens are played similarly to connectors preflop. You want to play them in late position when you can see the flop cheaply and get a multiway pot. If there are several callers, you should call, but if the pot has been raised, meaning it will now cost you two bets to play, you can quietly muck the small pair. If you've already bet and the pot gets raised, you can call that extra bet as long as you feel that you won't get trapped and raised again.

Though a pair will only improve to a three of a kind hand about one time in eight, when it does, you'll be sitting with a big hand that can trap opponents for a lot of chips. If it doesn't improve and there are overcards on the flop, you probably have the worst of it and should fold against an opponent's bet. One rule of thumb here—no set, no bet.

JUNK HANDS

All other hands not shown in the above three categories should be folded. They are heavy underdogs with little chance of winning. If you're in the big blind and the pot is unraised, by all means take the flop for free. But if it costs you to see the flop, fold immediately. It's cheaper watching this round as a bystander.

OTHER CONSIDERATIONS

If you miss the flop and think that betting will cause your opponent to fold, make the play. Otherwise, don't throw chips at longshots. Save them for better spots.

Be careful playing flush and straight draws unless they're to the **nuts**—the best hand possible given the cards on board. For example, you don't want to play a straight draw if there is a flush draw on board, or if you have, say the 6-7 on a board of 7-8-9-10-X. Any opponent with a jack will bust you here. And given that many players like to play J-10, that 7-8-9 flop is dangerous to your hand.

X. NO-LIMIT HOLD'EM STRATEGY

In no-limit hold'em, your entire stack of chips is at risk on every single hand—as are those of your opponents. One big mistake and they're gone. In limit hold'em, one bet is only one bet. In no-limit, that one bet could be the defining moment of your game because it could be for all your chips. And that changes the way you play hands.

No-limit hold'em appears deceptively simple at first glance, but as you get deeper into the strategies and the situations that occur, you start to see the many complexities of the game.

STARTING HANDS

If you're the first player coming into the pot on the preflop, you generally want to enter the pot with a **standard raise**, three times the size of the big blind. So if the big blind is at $5, make your raise $15, and if it's $10, make your raise $30. The reason you don't make the raise two times the big blind is that you make it too easy for your opponents, particularly the big blind, to enter the pot cheaply with marginal hands, subjecting your hand to lucky draws from opponents who might not otherwise see the flop.

You want your preflop raises to consistently be three times the size of the big blind so that opponents get no extra information on the strength of your hand. Players that vary their preflop raises are sometimes announcing their hands.

And if your opponents limp in to see the flop and you have a raising hand, make it four times the big blind. There is now more money in the pot and you want to make it unprofitable for them to call with marginal cards.

The hammer of the big bet or the all-in bet in no-limit hold'em puts a lot of pressure on opponents who hold marginal hands as well as strong hands in which they don't have confidence. Even when opponents think you're bluffing, it costs chips for them to find out for sure, which is often a greater cost than they're willing to risk.

The Preflop: Early Position

The best starting cards in no-limit hold'em are the **premium hands**—pocket aces, kings, queens, jacks, A-K, and A-Q. In an unraised pot, bring these hands in for a standard raise in early position. Your goal is to narrow the field to one or two callers and either to win the pot right there when all players fold or to reduce the number of players who will see the flop.

If you have aces or kings, hopefully you'll get a caller or two, or even better a raiser. Then you'll raise right back the size of the pot or go in for all your chips if you get reraised. With queens and A-K, you can stand a raise to see the flop, but if the raise is for all your chips and you're not short-stacked, you may need to let these hands go. If you don't want your day finished with queens, you certainly don't want to go out on jacks or A-Q! If an opponent goes all-in when you hold J-J or A-Q, or even puts in a big raise, these are grounds for folding these hands.

If a player comes in raising before you, the aces and kings are automatic reraises and the non-premium hands are automatic folds. Lean towards calling with A-K and queens. If the raiser is tight, fold with A-Q and jacks; if the raiser is loose, raising or calling are both viable options. Remember, that no play is set in stone in no-limit hold'em. You need to judge hands on a situation by situation basis.

Pass on all other hands from early position, especially against an aggressive table. If the table is tight, or it's early in a tournament and there's little cost to enter the pot, you may take a flier on a hand now and then to mix it up.

Middle Position

In middle position, you can play more hands due to the simple fact that you have fewer players behind who can raise your bets. If there is a raise before your turn, consider folding all non-premium hands. You don't want to go into the flop as a big underdog, which this earlier position raise probably indicates. And if the raiser is tight, fold jacks and A-Q as well. If you have aces or kings, reraise and have no fear of getting all your chips in the middle. You can also reraise with queens and A-K, or you could just call.

If no one has raised in front of you, you will still play the premium hands for a raise and can add the second tier hands—eights, nines and tens, along with A-J, A-10, and K-Q to your list of raising hands. If you get reraised by a player behind you, consider throwing second tier hands away. These hands have value but against heavy betting, they're chip burners.

Of course, if your opponent is low on chips and moves in on the preflop, especially in a tournament, give him credit for holding lesser quality cards and be prepared to play all premium hands—but again, use judgment. When in doubt, go with your gut.

Late Position

In late position, if the pot has been raised in early position, reraise with A-A, K-K, Q-Q and A-K. If you get reraised, you may consider just calling with Q-Q and A-K, and if the raiser is tight and goes all-in, you probably want to release these hands. And you certainly do not want to be in that reraised pot with jacks, A-Q or anything less. With aces and kings, you're always ready to play for all the marbles preflop.

If the pot is raised in middle position, reraise with the top four hands, A-A, K-K, Q-Q, and A-K. How you play jacks and A-Q is a judgment call, but it may be safer to just call and see the flop.

If there has been no raiser in the pot, you can expand your starting hands to any pair, an ace with any other card, and any two cards 10 or higher, for example, Q-10 or K-J. Generally, it's best to come in raising. Most of the time, you'll win the blinds, which is good. If you get callers, you have some value to see the flop.

If you get aces or kings in late position, and you think you'll get a caller, raise. If not, it might be better to limp in. You don't get kings or aces often, and when you do, you want to make money on them.

You can also play suited connectors, such as 6-7, 7-8, 8-9, and 10-J, if you can see the flop cheaply.

The Blinds

The blinds have the advantage of going last in the first round of play but the big disadvantage of going first in all other rounds. Play the blinds according to the advice in the early position strategy section.

If a late position bettor continually raises you out of the pot when you're the big blind, then you have to take a stand at some point to keep him in line. You'd like to have two big cards or ace-anything to reraise with, but you can also do this with garbage. If you read him correctly, he'll fold and you've got *his* chips. Do this once or twice and you'll get his attention and respect.

If everyone folds to you in the small blind and you can see the flop cheaply, it's not a bad play. You may flop something pretty or check to the showdown and win with better garbage than your opponent.

If there is no raise and you're in the big blind, and you're not in a raising situation, always see if for free— don't make the mistake of folding!

THE FLOP

If you come in raising preflop, you want to continue playing aggressive. If you're first, bet regardless of what flops. Your opponent will probably fold and you've got the pot. If he calls and you don't improve, you might consider checking on the turn. If he raises you, it's a tough call, but you'll have to consider giving up the hand unless you feel you've got better. Now, if you're second, and he checks, bet out at him.

What if he bets into you? If you miss the flop, give him the pot. Since you've shown strength preflop, his bet on the flop means you're probably second-best.

When you have what you think is the best hand, your goal is to take the pot immediately, particularly when there are straight and flush draws possible, for example, two cards of the same suit are on the board. You don't want opponents playing for another card cheaply, making it, and then destroying you on a hand that shouldn't have even seen another card. If opponents are going to beat you, make them pay to do so.

However, if you have an absolute monster like a full house or quads, you want to keep players in and extract more bets out of them. Often, that means checking and hoping a free card gives them a bigger hand.

THE TURN

If you've played aggressively on the preflop and flop, and your opponent hasn't budged, you have to figure him for possible strength. It's time for you to look at what you think *he thinks* you have. If you're representing strength and playing tight, you have to give him credit for a strong hand and slow down your betting. If he checks, you check, and if you're first, check to him and see how he reacts.

THE RIVER

When you have a big hand that you're confident is the best, you want to get more chips into the pot. If you're last and there have been no bets, put the amount of chips in the pot you feel your opponent will call. If you're first, you have two options: check or bet. If your opponent is very aggressive or has been leading at the pot, you can consider checking and letting him bet, then going over the top of him with a raise to try and get more chips in the pot. You want to be careful not to move an opponent off a pot with a bet. Let your knowledge of how your opponent plays guide you.

When you have a strong hand but have doubts whether it's the best one out there, it's often better to check at the river, rather than bet and risk a big raise that you won't call. If your opponent checks, you'll see the showdown with no further cost. If he bets, you see what you want to do. Be careful about betting in an attempt to get an opponent to fold. He might raise you back or set you all in, and you'll be forced to muck your cards and give up your chips.

If you're going to bluff at the river, however, make sure it's for enough chips so that your opponent will be faced with a tough decision on whether to call.

CASH GAME STRATEGY

In cash games, you're not worried about blinds, because they're generally small, nor are you concerned with antes, because there aren't any. Your goal in a cash game is purely and simply to win chips. You don't care if you have more chips than other players, or less, as long as you finish playing with more of them than you started with. And then you have won money.

When you have a good session and win lots of chips, you can take them off the table and leave any time you want. The chips you play with can be converted to real profits at any time.

In a cash game, you play simply to win chips.

TOURNAMENT STRATEGY

In a tournament, your strategy boils down to one thing: Survival. Your goal is to hang in there and move up the ladder as players get eliminated so that you can get into the prize money. And finally, you want to get to the final table or be the champion.

In a tournament, chips are power. If you have a lot of them, take advantage of your superior chip count by bullying short stacks and timid players with aggressive betting and by stealing their blinds. Anytime you bet and compete against a smaller stack, he knows that if he goes to war with you for all his chips and loses, he's eliminated. It is difficult for short stacks to play back at you because you can break them. Conversely, when you're that smaller stack, you must tread carefully against bigger stacks because your tournament will be at stake if all the chips go in the middle.

If you get **low-stacked**—that is, your chip stack is less than five times the size of the big blind—then you need to make a play for all your chips at the very first opportunity. If the pot is unraised and you have an ace with any other card, two cards 10 or higher, or any pair, go all-in and hope for the best. You cannot afford to play passive here—calling is not an option—you need the blinds and antes to stay alive.

Ideally, you would like your stack size to be at least ten times the size of the big blind. Either you take risks or you will get **blinded out**—lose all or a majority of your chips to the gradual forced blind and ante bets by barely playing any hands!

The most fundamental no-limit play to get chips is called **stealing the blinds**. This is when you raise in late position when no one else has entered the pot so that opponents will fold and you can win the blinds without a fight. The best position to do this from is the button or the seat before the button. Often, the blinds will fold, giving you the pot uncontested. You don't want to make this play every time, because your opponents will catch on, but at the same time, if the blinds are going to give you the pot without a fight, well then, take it every time.

In all situations, if an opponent is short-stacked, give him credit for much less of a hand than you would normally expect and don't be afraid to play all premium hands for all of your opponent's chips. You can also consider playing back at him with any pair or two high cards if you have a lot of chips and a loss here won't make you low-stacked. Just as you would play all sorts of hands when your stack is desperately low, so would your opponent, so you can open up here and call an all-in bet with less of a hand.

Early Round Tournament Strategy

In the first few rounds of a tournament, the blinds are generally small, and the antes won't kick in until the third or fourth level. During these early rounds, there is little pressure on you to make any moves as the blinds won't make too much of a dent in your stack, at least not a critical dent. Your strategy here is to play conservatively, trying to win little pots when possible and avoiding big pots unless you think you have the winner. You don't want to risk your tournament on a foolish bluff.

Your goal is to increase your chips stack as the tournament progresses, hopefully to double up after three rounds.

Middle Round Tournament Strategy

The middle rounds of a tournament, around levels four to eight, is when players start getting eliminated at a more rapid pace. The blinds and antes are more expensive and this means you have to play more hands and take more chances.

If you're low-stacked, aggressive play and stealing blinds becomes more important to keep up with the costs of feeding blinds and antes into the pot. If you're big-stacked, you want to push around the weak players and small stacks and get more chips. You're looking to position yourself for the final table.

Late Round Tournament Strategy

If you've lasted into the later rounds, you've either made it into the money or are getting real close. Now you look forward, hoping to get to the final table and the bigger money. You want to pick up your game here and play your best poker. Avoid facing off in big pots or all-ins against stacks that can take you out—unless you've got the goods—but as always in a tournament, keep pushing your weight around against players that can be bullied.

Final Table

If you get to the final table, you have a real shot at winning, but you still have to get through the last players. If you're among the big stacks, avoid going to war against another big stack that can bust you or make you one of the small stacks. Use your big stack to put pressure on smaller stacks struggling to stay alive.

If you're low stacked, the blinds and antes are exerting tremendous pressure, leaving you with little choice but to find your best opportunity and then go after it for all your chips. Calling is not an option here.

Think before you make your moves, keeping in mind that every player eliminated means a big jump in prize money.

XI. ONLINE POKER

Playing poker on the internet has become hugely popular. There are now millions of players from around the world competing against one another on hundreds of sites! With a few clicks of your mouse, you can get in on the action too.

It's easy to get started playing online. You begin by choosing a site and going to its homepage. From there, the instructions will guide you through all the basics: How to set up a unique account and password, how to play for free, and how to deposit funds into your account so that you can play for real money.

There are some good things about online poker. Let's take a look and see what they are.

SEVEN ADVANTAGES OF ONLINE POKER
1. It's Convenient

At any time of the day or night, all you have to do is go over to your computer, log on to your poker site of choice, and off you go. You're playing! There is nothing easier than that. It doesn't matter what you are wearing—or not wearing!—or how you look. You don't have to travel to a cardroom and search for the right game; with thousands of players online at any time, there is always a game with the stakes you want to play, waiting for you.

2. It's Good Social Fun

Poker fires up that competitive spirit and is a great social outlet as well. You may not be able to see your opponents live, but that won't stop you from being able to communicate with them. Just as in a live game, you *can* interact with your tablemates through the chat windows.

3. Make Friends around the World

Internet poker is now a worldwide phenomenon and it is not uncommon to see players at your table from a variety of countries. Like everything else, you eventually strike up friendships and you never know, you may soon be visiting some of your internet poker buddies—or be receiving them. Many great friendships have started online.

4. It's Great Practice

Online poker moves much faster than regular live games so you get to see lots of hands and situations. You can practice skills that you'll be able to apply to your regular tournament or cash game.

5. Play for Money or Play for Free

You can play poker for free on pretty much every site, a service online poker rooms offer their customers so they can get acclimated to the software. Or, if you prefer, you can sign up and play for real money.

6. It's Profitable

Online players are generally much weaker than competitors you'll find in regular cash games, especially at the low limit games. This makes it very profitable for good players. If you're a really skilled player, it's more than a good way to make money, it's a great way to make a living!

7. It's Generally Safe

The main Internet poker sites are already established businesses with hundreds of thousands of satisfied customers. It is generally accepted that major sites provide games as honest as any poker room, if not more so.

QUICK ONLINE STRATEGY TIPS

Online players tend to play too many hands and see too many showdowns. You adjust by playing solid straightforward poker. Fold weak hands and play good ones aggressively. Avoid bluffing (you can't bluff players who won't fold!), and give less credit for loose opponents having strong hands.

Like poker played in any form and in any setting, learning how your opponents play and adjusting your strategy accordingly will bring you the most profits.

FIND OUT MORE

To find out more about playing on online poker sites, go to www.cardozapub.com.

XII. MONEY MANAGEMENT

Never gamble with money you cannot afford to lose, either financially or emotionally. Risking funds you need for rent, food, or other essentials is a foolish gamble. The short term possibilities of taking a loss are real, no matter how easy the game may appear, no matter how stacked the odds are in your favor.

Whether you're playing cash games or tournaments, the most important thing is to stay within your comfort zone and play at levels you can afford. You need to play at limits that won't stress you out or make you vulnerable. If rent money is due, get off the table and pay the rent. If you've got important bills, get them covered. You should only gamble with discretionary funds, "extra" money that you don't mind putting at risk and potentially losing.

And how much of that should you risk? Again, it is about comfort level. If it hurts to lose money, you shouldn't be at the poker table in the first place.

If you're smart with your money, at worst, you lose your table bankroll—exactly what you planned on risking before you hit the tables—and at best, you make a bundle of money and have a great time doing so. And if you never play over your head, you can never get into trouble.

This is sound money management advice. Follow it and you can never go wrong.

HOLD'EM GLOSSARY

Act: To bet, raise, fold, or check.

Active Player: Player still in competition for the pot.

Ante: Mandatory bet placed into the pot by all players before the cards are dealt.

Bet: Money wagered and placed into the pot.

Big Blind: The larger of two mandatory bets made by the player two seats to the left of the dealer button position.

Bluff: To bet or raise with an inferior hand for the purpose of intimidating opponents into folding their cards and making the bluffer a winner by default.

Board: The face-up cards shared by all players. Also *Community Cards*.

Button: The player occupying the dealer position who goes last in all rounds except the preflop; also the disk used to indicate this position.

Buy-In: A player's investment of chips in a poker game or the actual amount of cash he or she uses to "buy" chips for play.

Call: To match an amount equal to a previous bet on a current round of betting.

Check: The act of "not betting" and passing the bet option to the next player while still remaining an active player.

Check and Raise: A player's raising of a bet after already checking in that round.

Community Cards: The face up cards shared by all players. Also *Board*.

Dealer: The player or casino employee who shuffles the cards and deals them out to the players.

Face Down: A card positioned such that its rank and suit faces the table and cannot be viewed by competing players. Cards dealt this way are also known as *Downcards*.

Face Up: A card positioned such that its rank and suit faces up and is therefore visible to all players. Cards dealt this way are also known as *Upcards* or *Open Cards*.

Flop: The first three cards simultaneously dealt face up for community use by all active players.

Flush: Hand containing five cards of the same suit.

Fold: Get rid of one's cards, thereby becoming inactive in the current hand and ineligible to play for the pot.

Four-of-a-Kind: Hand containing four cards of identical value, such as 9-9-9-9, four nines.

Free Card: A betting round where all players have checked, thereby allowing players to proceed to the next round of play without cost.

Full House: Hand consisting of three cards in one rank and two in another, such a 7-7-7-Q-Q.

Hand: The cards a player holds; the best five cards a player can present.

Head-to-Head: Hand or game played by two players only, one against the other. Also *Heads-Up.*

Hole Cards: Card held by a player whose value is hidden from other players.

Limit Poker: Betting structure in which the minimum and maximum bet sizes are set at fixed amounts, usually in a two-tiered structure such as $5-$10.

Limp: Call a bet as a way to enter the pot cheaply.

No-Limit: Betting structure in which the maximum bet allowed is limited only by the amount of money the bettor has on the table.

One Pair: Hand containing two cards of the same rank, such as Q-Q or 7-7.

Overcard: A hole card higher in rank than any board card. For example, a jack is an overcard to a flop of 10-6-2.

Pocket Cards: The two face-down cards received by all players.

Position: A player's relative position to the player acting last in a poker round.

Pot: The sum total of all antes, blinds, and bets placed in the center of the table by players during a poker hand.

Pot-Limit: Betting structure in which the largest bet can be no more than the current size of the pot.

Preflop: The first betting round in hold'em, when each player has only their two pocket cards.

Premium Starting Hands: One in a group of the best starting cards in hold'em: A-A, K-K, Q-Q and A-K and sometimes A-Q and J-J as well.

Raise: A wager that increases a previous bet.

Rake: The amount of money taking out of the pot by the house as its fee for running the game.

Reraise: To raise another player's raise.

Ring Game: A cash game with a full table of players, usually seven or more.

River: The fifth community card on board.

Royal Flush: An A-K-Q-J-10 of the same suit. The highest ranking hand in hold'em.

Set: Three of a kind.

Shorthanded: A poker game played with six players or less.

Showdown: The final act in a poker game, where remaining players reveal their hands to determine the winner of the pot.

Small Blind: The smaller of two mandatory bets made by the player sitting immediately to the left of the dealer button position.

Standard Raise: A preflop raise of three times the big blind.

Steal the Blinds: On the first betting round, bluff opponents out of a pot no one has entered so that the blinds can be won.

Straight: A sequence of five consecutive cards of mixed suits, such as 4-5-6-7-8.

Straight Flush: A sequence of five consecutive cards in the same suit, such as 8-9-10-J-Q all of spades.

Table Stakes: A rule stating that a player's bet or call of a bet is limited to the amount of money he has on the table in front of him.

Three of a Kind: Poker hand containing three cards of the same rank, such as 4-4-4.

Tournament: A competition in which players start with an equal number of chips and play until one player holds all them.

Trips: Three of a kind.

Turn: The fourth community card on board.

Two Pair: Poker hand containing two sets of two cards of the same rank, such as J-J-5-5.

Under the Gun: The first player to act in a round of poker.

WPT: World Poker Tour.

WSOP: World Series of Poker.

THE CHAMPIONSHIP SERIES
POWERFUL BOOKS YOU MUST HAVE

HOW TO WIN NO-LIMIT HOLD'EM TOURNAMENTS *by Tom McEvoy. & Don Vines.* Learn the basic concepts of tournament strategy, plus how to win big by playing small buy-in events, how to graduate to medium and big buy-in tournaments; how to adjust for short fields, huge fields, slow and fast-action events, plus how to win online no-limit tournaments; manage a tournament bankroll, and tips on table demeanor for televised tournaments. See actual hands played by finalists at WSOP and WPT championship tables with card pictures, analysis and useful lessons from the play. 376 pages, $29.95

CHAMPIONSHIP WIN YOUR WAY INTO BIG MONEY HOLD'EM TOURNAMENTS *by Brad Dougherty & Tom McEvoy.* Every year, from 2002 to 2005, satellite players won their way into the $10,000 WSOP buy-in and emerged as millionaires or champions. You can too! You'll learn specific, proven strategies for winning almost any satellite. Covers the 10 ways to win a seat at the WSOP, how to win limit hold'em and no-limit hold'em satellites, one-table satellites, online satellites, plus the final table of super satellites. Includes a special chapter on no-limit hold'em satellites! 320 pages, $29.95.

CHAMPIONSHIP HOLD'EM TOURNAMENT HANDS *by T. J. Cloutier & Tom McEvoy.* An absolute must for hold'em tournament players, two legends show you how to become a winning tournament player at both limit and no-limit hold'em games. Get inside their heads as they think they way through the correct strategy at 57 limit and no-limit starting hands. Cloutier & McEvoy show you how to use skill and intuition to play strategic hands for maximum profit in real tournament scenarios and how 45 key hands were played by champions in turnaround situations at the WSOP. Gain tremendous insights into how tournament poker is played at the highest levels. 368 pages, $29.95

CHAMPIONSHIP TOURNAMENT POKER *by Tom McEvoy.* Enthusiastically endorsed by more than 5 world champions, this is a *must* for every player's library. McEvoy lets you in on the secrets he has used to win millions of dollars in tournaments and the insights he has learned competing against the best players in the world. Packed solid with winning strategies for 11 games with extensive discussions of 7-card stud, limit hold'em, pot and no-limit hold'em, Omaha high-low, re-buy, half-half tournaments, satellites, strategies for each stage of tournaments. 416 pages, $29.95.

CHAMPIONSHIP TABLE (at the World Series of Poker) *by Dana Smith, Ralph Wheeler, and Tom McEvoy. Championship Table* celebrates three decades of poker greats who have competed to win poker's most coveted title. This book gives you the names and photographs of all the players who made the final table, pictures the last hand the champion played against the runner-up, how they played their cards, how much they won, plus fascinating interviews and conversations with the champions. This fascinating and invaluable resource book includes tons of vintage photographs. 208 pages, $19.95.

THE CHAMPIONSHIP SERIES
POWERFUL BOOKS YOU MUST HAVE

CHAMPIONSHIP HOLD'EM *by T. J. Cloutier & Tom McEvoy.* Hard-hitting hold'em the way it's played *today* in both limit cash games and tournaments. Get killer advice on how to win more money in rammin'-jammin' games, kill-pot, jackpot, shorthanded, and other types of cash games. You'll learn the thinking process before the flop, on the flop, on the turn, and at the river with specific suggestions for what to do when good or bad things happen plus 20 illustrated hands with play-by-play analyses. Specific advice for rocks in tight games, weaklings in loose games, experts in solid games, how hand values change in jackpot games, when you should fold, check, raise, reraise, check-raise, slowplay, bluff, and tournament strategies for small buy-in, big buy-in, rebuy, incremental add-on, satellite and big-field major tournaments. Wow! If you want to win at limit hold'em, you need this book! 392 pages, $29.95

CHAMPIONSHIP NO-LIMIT & POT-LIMIT HOLD'EM *by T. J. Cloutier & Tom McEvoy.* This is the bible of winning pot-limit and no-limit hold'em tournaments. You'll get all the answers here —no holds barred—to your most important questions: How do you get inside your opponents' heads and learn how to beat them at their own game? How can you tell how much to bet, raise, and reraise in no-limit hold'em? When can you bluff? How do you set up your opponents in pot-limit hold'em so that you can win a monster pot? What are the best strategies for winning no-limit and pot-limit tournaments, satellites, and supersatellites? Rock-solid and inspired advice you can bank on from two of the most recognizable figures in poker. 304 pages, $29.95

CHAMPIONSHIP OMAHA (Omaha High-Low, Pot-limit Omaha, Limit High Omaha) *by T. J. Cloutier & Tom McEvoy.* Clearly-written strategies and powerful advice from Cloutier and McEvoy who have won four World Series of Poker titles in Omaha tournaments. Powerful advice shows you how to win at low-limit and high-stakes games, how to play against loose and tight opponents, and the differing strategies for rebuy and freezeout tournaments. Learn the best starting hands, when slowplaying a big hand is dangerous, what danglers are and why winners don't play them, why pot-limit Omaha is the only poker game where you sometimes fold the nuts on the flop and are correct in doing so and overall, how can you win a lot of money at Omaha! 230 pages, photos, illustrations, $29.95.

CHAMPIONSHIP STUD (Seven-Card Stud, Stud 8/or Better and Razz) *by Dr. Max Stern, Linda Johnson, and Tom McEvoy.* The authors, who have earned millions of dollars in major tournaments and cash games, eight World Series of Poker bracelets and hundreds of other titles in competition against the best players in the world show you the winning strategies for medium-limit side games as well as poker tournaments and a general tournament strategy that is applicable to any form of poker. Includes give-and-take conversations between the authors to give you more than one point of view on how to play poker. 200 pages, hand pictorials, photos. $29.95.